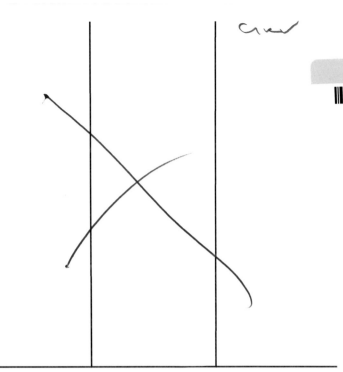

Books should be returned or renewed by the last
date above. Renew by phone **03000 41 31 31** or
online *www.kent.gov.uk/libs*

C334477422

Grace Hopper

The Woman Behind Computer Programming

Nancy Loewen

raintree
a Capstone company — publishers for children

Raintree is an imprint of Capstone Global Library Limited, a company incorporated in England and Wales having its registered office at 264 Banbury Road, Oxford, OX2 7DY – Registered company number: 6695582

www.raintree.co.uk
myorders@raintree.co.uk

Editor: Jill Kalz
Designer: Kayla Rossow
Media researcher: Svetlana Zhurkin
Original illustrations © Capstone Global Library Limited 2020
Production Specialist: Tori Abraham
Originated by Capstone Global Library Ltd
Printed and bound in India

ISBN 978 1 4747 8676 8 (hardback)
ISBN 978 1 4747 8682 9 (paperback)

British Library Cataloguing in Publication Data
A full catalogue record for this book is available from the British Library.

Acknowledgements
We would like to thank for the following for permission to use photographs: Alamy: John Frost Newspapers, 17, RBM Vintage Images, 13 (top), Science History Images, 21; Library of Congress, 7, 8, 24; National Archives and Records Administration: DVIC, 5 (top), 26, 28; Newscom: akg-images, 11 (top), Everett Collection, 19 (bottom), 25, Mirrorpix/Daily Mirror, 9, UIG/Underwood Archives, 16; Science Source: cover, 23 (bottom), New York Public Library, 13 (bottom); Shutterstock: Africa Studio, 6, Everett Historical, 10, Samuel Borges Photography, 4; Smithsonian Institution: National Museum of American History, 22, 27, National Museum of American History, Archives Center, Grace Murray Hopper Collection, 1944-1965, 11 (bottom), 12, 14, 15 (top), National Museum of American History/Transfer from United States Department of Defense, Naval Surface Warfare Center, 15 (bottom), National Portrait Gallery/Photo (c) Lynn Gilbert, 29 (bottom); U.S. Navy: Mass Communication Specialist 2nd Class Alexander Ventura II, 29 (top); Wikimedia Commons: 5 (bottom), Alejandro Quintanar, 19 (top), Department of Defense, 23 (top). Design Elements by Shutterstock.

Our very special thanks to Emma Grahn, Spark!Lab Manager, Lemelson Center for the Study of Invention and Innovation, National Museum of American History, USA, for her invaluable help in the preparation of this book. We would also like to thank Kealy Gordon, Product Development Manager, and the following at Smithsonian Enterprises: Ellen Nanney, Licensing Manager; Brigid Ferraro, Vice President, Education and Consumer Products; and Carol LeBlanc, Senior Vice President, Education and Consumer Products.

CONTENTS

INTRODUCTION

Have you ever played games on a smartphone? Looked up something on a computer? Watched a film on a tablet? Then you can thank Grace Hopper!

Hopper was a pioneer in computer programming. Clever and curious, she never stopped looking for a problem to solve. Her amazing inventions benefit people round the world every day.

All of today's computer devices are linked to Hopper's work.

The Grace Hopper Celebration of Women in Computing event is held every year. It's the world's largest gathering of women who work in technology.

Grace Hopper spent 43 years in the US Navy.

After her death, Hopper received the Presidential Medal of Freedom from former US President Barack Obama. The medal is the highest civilian honour given in the United States.

OFF TO A GOOD START

Grace was born in 1906 to Walter and Mary Murray in New York City, USA. She was always curious about how things worked. At the age of seven she took apart the family's clocks to see their insides.

Grace was rejected at first by Vassar College aged 16. Her scores in Latin were too low. She was accepted the following year.

The insides of a clock

At that time, many people believed that education was more important for boys than girls. Grace's parents didn't agree. They sent their daughter to good schools. They told her to work hard. She earned university degrees in mathematics and physics at Vassar College. Then she went to Yale University. There she earned a PhD in maths at the age of 28.

Grace studied, slept and ate in Vassar's Main Building.

Grace married Vincent Hopper, an English professor, in 1930. They divorced in 1945.

A TERRIFIC TEACHER

Hopper was more than a good student. She was also a terrific teacher. After earning her PhD, she went back to Vassar College to teach maths. She taught there for more than 10 years.

It wasn't unusual for wealthy women to go to university during Hopper's time. But it *was* unusual for married women to teach.

Vassar is a top US university. Between 1861 and 1969 it only took women.

Albert Einstein used maths to explain his ideas about matter and energy.

Hopper liked to teach scientist Albert Einstein's "new and exciting" work in her classes.

At Vassar College, teachers could go to any class for free. Hopper sat in on lots of classes. She took her ideas to her students. She wanted to inspire them. She saw maths as a link across all areas of study.

TURNING POINT

World War II (1939–1945) changed everything for Hopper. She wanted to serve in the US Navy. But at the age of 35, she was considered too old. She didn't weigh enough either.

The Japanese attack on Pearl Harbor, Hawaii, on 7 December 1941, pushed the United States to enter World War II.

Hopper's great-grandfather was an admiral in the Navy during the Civil War (1861–65).

Hopper didn't give up. She convinced the Navy to let her in anyway. In December 1943 she joined the WAVES (Women Accepted for Volunteer Emergency Service). The programme was part of the Navy Reserves. In 1944 she became a lieutenant.

Members of WAVES helped build and fix aeroplanes for the Navy during World War II.

Hopper graduated first in her class from the Naval Reserve Midshipmen's School at Smith College in 1944.

A MATHEMATICAL ROBOT

The Navy sent Hopper to Harvard University. Her job was to work with a machine called Mark I. It was used to solve hard maths problems. Mark I wasn't like today's computers. It was huge! It used paper tape with punched holes. The pattern of the holes was called code. The code told the computer what to do.

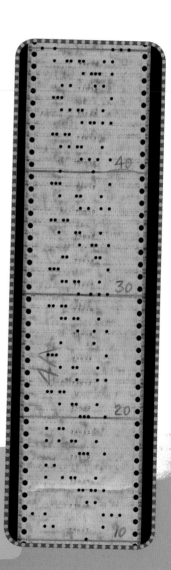

Some of the first computers got their instructions from patterns of holes punched out of rolls of paper tape.

Mark I was sometimes called the "Mathematical Robot". It was built by the company IBM.

Mark I was 16 metres (51 feet) long, 2m (8 ft) high, and 1m (3 ft) wide. It had 853 kilometres (530 miles) of wiring.

Hopper used a keyboard to enter code onto a paper tape.

The problems Mark I solved were mostly about the war. Everything was top secret. Often Hopper didn't even know how her work was used.

THE RIGHT WOMAN FOR THE JOB

During World War II, Mark I ran 24 hours a day. Hopper put in long hours in her job. Sometimes she slept at her desk. She was the only woman in the Mark I team. Some of the men didn't think a woman belonged there. Hopper soon changed their minds! She worked hard and was good at getting the best out of the team.

Later known as "Amazing Grace", Hopper pioneered the way for women in computer programming.

Hopper wrote a 561-page manual for Mark I.

Mark I worked almost non-stop for 16 years.

After the war, Hopper stayed at Harvard. She helped design the next computers, Mark II and Mark III.

A COMPUTER BUG

Grace Hopper wasn't the first person to call a problem a "bug". But she may have been the first to apply it to computing. One day the Mark II computer stopped working. Hopper and her team found a dead moth in it. For fun, Hopper taped the moth into her log book. "The first actual case of a bug being found," she wrote. The moth is now at the National Museum of American History.

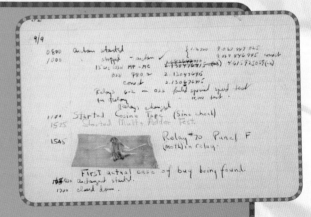

NEW GROWTH

Only the government used the Mark computers. Some people thought they could be used by businesses too. Grace Hopper was one of those people.

The UNIVAC filled a room and weighed about 7 tons.

In the 1950s the word *UNIVAC* meant "computer" to most people. UNIVAC stood for Universal Automatic Computer.

In 1949 Hopper took a job at a computer company in Pennsylvania. The company made a computer called the UNIVAC. Like any new invention, the UNIVAC had problems. It was big. It cost a lot. And it was difficult to use.

The UNIVAC was challenged to pick who would win the 1952 US presidential election. After programmers loaded the data, the room-size computer said Dwight D. Eisenhower would win. And he did.

HOPPER'S GREAT IDEA

Hopper was always trying to solve problems. She wanted better, faster ways to do things. For years she had been collecting bits of code that she often used. In 1952 she took these bits and put them on a tape. Each bit was given a call number. The computer brought up the call number. Then it could use all the code already in the system.

Hopper had invented the first compiler. It was a shortcut. And it worked!

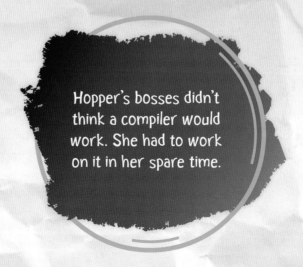

Hopper's bosses didn't think a compiler would work. She had to work on it in her spare time.

Inside the UNIVAC lay a maze of wires, tubes and other electronic parts.

Before Hopper's compiler, all computer programs were built from scratch - even if they shared much of the same code. The process took a lot of time. Mistakes were often made.

The UNIVAC stored information on magnetic tape.

THE POWER OF WORDS

Hopper's next challenge also involved code. At the time only maths experts could be programmers. They wrote code using numbers and other maths symbols. Hopper thought code could be written with words. If a machine could read a symbol, why couldn't it read a letter? She thought code based on words would be more user-friendly.

Hopper kept a clock in her office that ran backwards. It reminded her that most problems can be solved in many ways, not just one.

```
(14) SET OPERATION 4 TO GO TO
OPERATION 5.
(15) JUMP TO OPERATION 5.
READ-ITEM A; IF END OF DATA GO
TO OPERATION 16.
(16) TEST PRODUCT; IF EQUAL GO
TO OPERATION 18; OTHERWISE GO TO
OPERATION 17.
(17) TRANSFER A TO D. REWIND B.
```

An example of word-based code

In 1951 one UNIVAC cost more than £7 million in today's pounds (2019 estimate).

Hopper and her team made another compiler. This one used common business words. Called FLOW-MATIC, the compiler helped companies pay workers, send bills and do many other tasks.

FLOW-MATIC was in use by 1956.

A TEAM PLAYER

FLOW-MATIC was a success. But Hopper wanted to push herself even more. She wanted to create one standard language for every computer in the world.

Hopper gathered a large team of programmers. Together they created COBOL. It stood for Common Business-oriented Language. The new language could "talk" to all computers. COBOL came out in 1959. It is still used today.

Hopper understood the importance of working as a team.

Today 80 per cent of all daily business dealings around the world use COBOL.

COBOL

Report to
CONFERENCE on DATA SYSTEMS LANGUAGES

Including
INITIAL SPECIFICATIONS for a COMMON BUSINESS ORIENTED LANGUAGE (COBOL) for Programming Electronic Digital Computers

DEPARTMENT OF DEFENSE   APRIL 1960

"If you ask me what accomplishment I'm proudest of, the answer would be all the young people I've trained over the years; that's more important than writing the first compiler."

—Grace Hopper

Hopper quickly became the face of the new language called COBOL.

GAME CHANGER

Hopper's work was quickly changing the computer world. It was also changing the business world. People began to understand that hardware and software were two different things. Lots of different programs could run on the same machines. People could more easily share what they learned. Progress could happen faster.

In 1969 Hopper was named computer science's "Man of the Year"!

Grace Hopper in around 1961

In the 1960s computers helped businesses to print reports.

During her lifetime, Hopper published more than 50 articles about computing.

"GRANDMA COBOL"

Hopper worked with computers for the rest of her life. She taught classes and helped businesses solve problems. In her later years, she was a popular speaker. People liked her funny stories and sayings. They liked how she challenged them to try new ideas.

Known as "Grandma COBOL", Hopper inspired many young people to dream big.

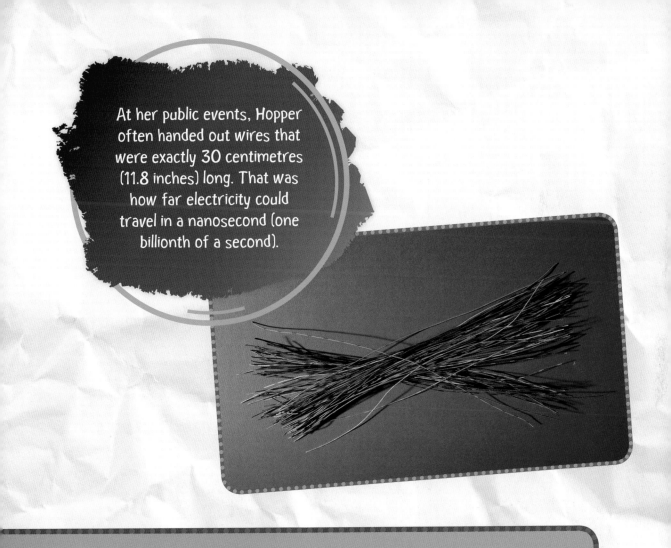

At her public events, Hopper often handed out wires that were exactly 30 centimetres (11.8 inches) long. That was how far electricity could travel in a nanosecond (one billionth of a second).

IN THE NAVY

Grace Hopper's career in the US Navy lasted for 43 years. She served in the Navy Reserve from 1943 until 1966, when she was forced to retire because of her age. But the following year, the Navy called her into special service to help solve computer problems. She remained in the Navy until 1986. When she finally retired for real, she was the oldest active officer and had achieved the rank of rear admiral. Her retirement celebration was held aboard the USS *Constitution,* the Navy's oldest ship.

NEVER FORGOTTEN

Grace Hopper died in 1992 at the age of 85. Her inventions made possible many later developments in computer programming. They made computers more user-friendly. Computer languages run our banks, our shops, our governments . . . even our computer games! And they all draw from the amazing work of Grace Hopper.

Hopper was buried with full military honours at Arlington National Cemetery in Virginia.

The Navy named a warship after Grace Hopper – the USS *Hopper*.

"When you have a good idea and you've tried it and you know it's going to work, go ahead and do it — because it's much easier to apologize afterwards than it is to get permission."

—Grace Hopper

One of Hopper's lasting lessons is that great ideas and teamwork can meet any challenge.

GLOSSARY

code system of symbols for sending messages

degree title given by a university when a student completes a programme of study

hardware physical parts of a computer

inspire to cause someone to want to do something positive

military to do with the armed forces

Navy branch of the armed forces that operate at sea

Navy Reserve branch of the US Navy in which people serve part-time

PhD highest degree a person can earn from a university; also called a doctorate. "PhD" stands for "Doctor of Philosophy".

pioneer person who is one of the first to try new things

programmer person who writes the code that tells computers what to do

software set of instructions that gives computers particular tasks

symbol something that stands for something else (such as a "+" that means "add")

university place of study in which people gain degrees and carry out research

COMPREHENSION QUESTIONS

1. What were some of the ways Grace Hopper changed the world of computers?

2. Hopper thought it was important to work well with others. How do you think that affected what she was able to do?

3. From the beginning, Hopper believed that computers would be important in our daily lives. Was she right? How are computers used in daily life?

FIND OUT MORE

Grace Hopper: Queen of Computer Code (People Who Shaped Our World), Laurie Wallmark (Sterling, 2017)

Grace Hopper (Women in Science and Technology), Jan Fields (Discovery Library, 2019)

Technology: Cool Women Who Code (Girls in Science), Andi Diehn (Nomad Press, 2015)

Women in Science: 50 Fearless Pioneers Who Changed the World, Rachel Ignotofsky (Wren & Rook, 2017)

WEBSITES

An animated video-biography of Grace Hopper
www.youtube.com/watch?v=Fg82iV-L8ZY

Grace Hopper talks about nanoseconds
www.youtube.com/watch?v=JEpsKnWZrJ8

INDEX